D0340791

Dear Saint Anne, Send Me a Man

Dear Saint Anne, Send Me a Man

(And other time-honored prayers for love)

Alice La Plante & Clare La Plante

Illustrations by Timothy Basil Ering

UNIVERSE

HOUSTON PUBLIC LIBRARY

R01278 67224

First published in the United States of America in 2002
by UNIVERSE PUBLISHING
A Division of Rizzoli International Publications, Inc.
300 Park Avenue South
New York, NY 10010

Copyright © 2001 by Alice La Plante and Clare La Plante

All rights reserved. No part of this publication may be
reproduced, stored in a retrieval system, or transmitted in
any form or by any means, electronic, mechanical, photo-
copying, recording, or otherwise, without prior consent of
the publisher.

Printed in Singapore

Library of Congress Control Number: 2001094241

Design by Davidson Design
Illustrations © Timothy Basil Ering

2001 2002 2003 2004 2005 / 10 9 8 7 6 5 4 3 2 1

Acknowledgments

IT WOULDN'T BE POSSIBLE TO PERSONALLY THANK everyone who helped us with this book. We do, however, want to express our special gratitude to the following people.

Our fabulous agent, Arielle Eckstut of James Levine Communications, came through for us yet again, delivering her usual expert guidance with humor and enthusiasm. She inspires us. For her intelligent shaping and editing of the text, we thank our editor Kathleen Jayes. We would have followed Kathleen anywhere, but are delighted that her path led us to Universe/Rizzoli.

Timothy Basil Ering's talent and whimsical sense of joy shines through every drawing. Our designer Karen Davidson provided the perfect frame for Timothy's work.

Special thanks as well to our families and friends who supported us during the writing and researching of this book.

Saintly Intervention in Matters of Love

An Introduction

WITHIN MONTHS OF THE RELEASE OF OUR FIRST BOOK about patron saints (*Heaven Help Us: The Worrier's Guide to the Patron Saints*), we began to hear stories about St. Anne.

Because St. Anne gave birth to Mary, mother of Jesus, after years of unsuccessful efforts to have a child, generations have turned to her for help with a wide range of what you might call "women's issues": marriage, conception, childbirth, parenting, and—of course—love. We had included many rituals associated with St. Anne in *Heaven Help Us* but one, apparently, struck a nerve: a simple chant to help women searching for a mate: "Dear Saint Anne, send me a man."

Suddenly we were hearing everyone's Saint Anne stories. The first testimony to St. Anne's matchmaking abilities came from the daughter of a friend of our mother who appealed to Saint Anne for help in love. One day she came home to find her answering machine filled with messages from eager would-be suitors. The second St. Anne story came from a woman who chanted "Dear Saint Anne, send me a man" for two straight days until the crush of her life came up to her and finally asked her out. Another woman, a doubting Thomas sort, sheepishly confessed that she had been saying St. Anne's prayer. What did she have to lose after all? She found true love—and marriage—shortly thereafter.

Or there was the group of women who, inspired by our book, organized a pilgrimage to the Shrine of Saint Anne (*which is located in Chicago, by the way*) to say a prayer or two and perhaps get a little closer to the source. No word yet on the romantic results, but they have high hopes that Saint Anne will come through.

By the way, in case you think it's just women who are seeking love, we'd like gently to prove you wrong. We heard from a young man who, in desperation, has been chanting "Dear Saint Abe, send me a babe; Dear Saint Nick, send me a chick." Okay, so there's no Saint Abe. But we give this guy a lot of credit for trying.

What all this shows is that love still makes the world go round. But in this rushed and harried age, it can be tough to find a date for New Year's Eve—not to mention your soul mate. Sometimes you just need a little help. And that's where this book comes in. For St. Anne isn't alone in her romantic patronage. Instead she is part of a whole host of heavenly helpers who have a soft spot for lovelorn mortals, and they are just waiting for us to call upon them for aid. For however hierarchical the Catholic church may appear, it is in fact a composite of the many people in it (that's the "catholic" part of it). This communion of souls includes everyone who has ever lived, including, of course, the saints. It's a lot like how Buddhists turn to their ancestors—they're not dead, per se, they're just not walking the earth, and they are still available to us.

We wrote this book in this spirit of helpful community. Consider it your indispensable guide to the love experts: those who have seen it all, heard it all, and actually want to help. After all, they must be doing something right. They've been on the job for hundreds, even thousands, of years.

Oh yes, we knew you were going to ask: do the prayers work? We say: as well as the hearts and desires that guide them.

Curious about who you'll marry? (Or who you'll marry next?) Perhaps you're just looking for a date for the office Christmas party? This section introduces the saints who specialize in various forms of divination. While most of the glimpses of your future mate will be afforded through guest-starring roles in your dreams, be prepared for other ghostly apparitions, including sudden appearances in your bathroom mirror.

Saints Who Can Predict Your Romantic Future

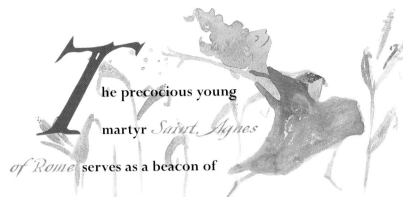

The precocious young martyr *Saint Agnes of Rome* serves as a beacon of hope to the lovelorn by bestowing visions of future mates to both men and women.

Agnes is one of the most beloved of a special category of female saints known as the "virgin martyrs." Like all martyrs, these holy women—and they were all women—were killed because of their faith.

The definition of a martyr is someone who chooses to die rather than betray a religious conviction, and all Christian martyrs are automatically made saints upon their death—no other qualifications necessary.

The special twist for a virgin martyr such as Agnes is that her efforts to defend her faith were inextricably linked with her struggles to keep her chastity intact. Many of the virgin martyrs were nuns, or otherwise had taken vows that made them "brides of Christ." Celibacy in such cases became inseparable from other religious duties.

Agnes's story is unique because of the passion she inspired despite her very young age, and the extreme lengths to which her persecutors went to tempt and torment her. Only a child of twelve or thirteen when she died (St. Ambrose says twelve years old, St. Augustine, thirteen—even holy men seem to have this need to compile statistics, and bicker about them), Agnes already had fended off a number of seductions from an impressive line-up of would-be husbands. Thus in art, Agnes is represented by a lamb, the symbol of her virginity and innocence.

There are many versions of Agnes's story, but we like the one featuring a bratty young nobleman called Eutropius, who happened to be the son of the local Roman governor. Eutropius was apparently one of those guys who thinks "no" means "OK," because he continued to pester Agnes despite her assertions that she was already in a committed relationship with a much worthier suitor—Christ. Eutropius whined for so long and so hard that his royal father became irritated enough to offer Agnes unimaginable wealth and power if she would only agree to become his daughter-in-law and help silence his callow son. No dice, Agnes said.

Not surprisingly, Eutropius Senior was affronted by her refusal, and so after the carrot came a very big stick: Agnes was taken to the royal dungeon and tortured in ways that would have broken much stronger and braver individuals. Bloody but unbowed, Agnes refused to even consider renouncing her vows to Christ. After all else failed, father and son joined forces to strip Agnes naked, cut off her hair, and parade her into the town square for public humiliation. It was then that the first miracle attributed to Agnes occurred: her shorn hair immediately grew back to cover her nakedness before any of the townspeople could catch a glimpse of her in an indecent state. Undaunted by this sign that Agnes was under God's protection, the two royal louts, father and son, ordered her taken to the most notorious brothel in town, there to be pawed over and violated by local yokels.

But here the second miracle occurred: at the entrance to the brothel, an angel appeared and placed a beautiful shimmering white garment around Agnes that no one could remove. It was at this point that Eutropius's daddy apparently went bananas. Forgetting that he was, after all, trying to help his son, Eutropius Senior proclaimed loudly that no one would have Agnes but himself. With this, he tried to embrace her. Again the angel, who had apparently been expecting something of this sort, came to Agnes's aid by blinding the governor. Agnes was so moved by Eutropius Senior's suffering—there's no record of what his betrayed son was thinking—that she asked God to restore the older man's sight. Naturally, God did so immediately, and equally naturally, the governor rewarded Agnes by ordering his soldiers to kill her on the spot. Agnes was overjoyed to hear his command, knowing her suffering would soon end and she would be with her true Beloved, Jesus.

After her death, Agnes's body was placed in a separate sepulchre on the Via Nomentana, where a basilica, or small church, was erected during Constantine's reign. You can still view the original slab on which Agnes's body rested at the Museum of Naples.

There are a number of versions of the Agnes legend—you are likely to hear, for example, that after rejecting her umpteenth suitor, the young but irresistible Agnes was killed while on her mother's lap.

Other versions have her burned to death, or decapitated by sword. Most of the Agnes stories you hear, however, will include some variation of her public march to the brothel.

Perhaps it is her faith in the face of public humiliation that encourages lovers to ask for her aid—after all, what's more fraught with embarrassment than dating? Most of the rituals involving Agnes require some form of fasting for a specified length of time in order to get a glimpse of a future spouse. Called "fasting St. Agnes's fast," this ritual is frequently referred to in literature—the following happens to be by Shakespeare's contemporary, Ben Johnson:

> *And on sweet St. Agnes' night*
> *Please you with the promis'd sight*
> *Some of husbands, some of lovers,*
> *Which an empty dream discovers.*

To ask St. Agnes to intervene for you, try one of the following rituals. Most rituals involving St. Agnes come from England, where women and men alike would ask her to intercede on their behalf to get a glimpse of future love. As with most saint-related rituals, the following should theoretically be performed on the eve of her feast day, in this case January 20, since Agnes's official feast day is January 21. However, we have heard that invokers have had success on other nights. We think that if you petition her in the right spirit, lovely Agnes will be sure to listen.

Here's what you do:

1. Take a handful of straight pins—about a dozen should do.
2. Stick them in one of your sleeves.
3. Pull them out, one at a time, saying a Paternoster *(Our Father)* after each one.
4. After you're done with your Our Fathers, say the following:

Fair St. Agnes, play thy part
And send to me my own sweetheart,
Not in his best nor worst array,
But in the clothes he wears every day;
That tomorrow I may him ken,
From among all other men.

What you can expect:

That night you will dream of the man or woman you will marry. *(Try to wake yourself up if you see the visage of Regis Philbin or Roseanne Barr beginning to form.)*

Here's a slightly weirder ritual for those who have a more… earthy… sense of humor.

Here's what you do:

1. Take a sprig of rosemary, a spring of thyme, and sprinkle both with urine—yes, that's right, although whose isn't specified.

2. Do this three times.
3. Then take a pair of your shoes, preferably ones you don't wear to the office. Place the scented rosemary *(ahhh!)* in one of the shoes, and the thyme in the other shoe.
4. Put the shoes on either side of your bed.
5. Say the following prayer:

St. Agnes who to lovers kind
Come ease the trouble of my mind

Another version of this prayer is as follows:

St. Agnes Day comes by and by
When pretty maids do fast to try
Their sweethearts in their dreams to see
Or know who shall their husbands be.

What you can expect:

That night you will dream of the man or woman you will marry. We're not sure if this is more accurate than the other rituals. But it does seem as though there should be some extra payoff for potentially ruining a good pair of shoes. At least your dog should be happy.

Finally, one last ritual, but a more difficult one to perform, as it requires a cornfield. Also, you'll need a couple of handfuls of loose grain. Perhaps the produce aisle of your local supermarket will do? The way it's supposed to work is as follows.

Here's what you do:

1. At the stroke of midnight—okay, it's going to have to be a twenty-four-hour supermarket—you go into a cornfield, and throw some grain into it. *(Cheerios? Shredded Wheat?)*

2. After this, you pronounce as loudly as you can *(or as loudly as you dare)*:

> *Agnes, sweet and Agnes fair*
> *Hither, hither, now repair;*
> *Bonny Agnes, let me see*
> *The lad/maid who is to marry me.*

What you can expect:

When you get home, look in the mirror. You will see the shadow of your future bride or bridegroom there.

Saint Luke is a former physician with an impressive bedside manner: he gives you visions of your future love. Although most frequently petitioned in medieval times by women, today men should also feel welcome to avail themselves of Luke's help.

Luke is best known for his version of the gospel in the New Testament. Although Luke accompanied the apostle Paul on his early evangelical missions throughout the then-Roman world, Luke apparently didn't agree with the rather stringent views and dictums laid out in Paul's version of the gospel. Luke's gospel is gentler and more compassionate, and includes many of the best-known stories associated with Jesus, including "The Prodigal Son" and "The Good Samaritan."

In an effort to help early Christians more wholeheartedly embrace their new religion, church officials allowed them to continue with certain established pagan practices as long as a Christian saint was used as the point of reference.

There's no logical reason for Luke to have patronages in matters of romance and courtship. Rather, scholars believe that the love-related rituals associated with Luke come directly from pagan practices. Luke's feast day *(the day he died)* is October 18, which falls smack in the middle of traditional harvest activities. As medieval people were largely farmers and dependent on the agricultural calendar, the season was full of harvest-related festivities and rituals meant to celebrate the end of the growing year, and to ensure good luck for the next. Many outrageous and outright bawdy practices have therefore become attached to poor Luke, who would probably be bewildered by what has been done in his name for centuries.

To ask St. Luke to intervene for you, try the following ritual. Those wishing to have a vision of their future mate should try this one. Although it's a little messy, you can do it in the privacy of your own home. *(The rituals in which you face public scrutiny are definitely harder to pull off.)*

Here's what you do:

1. Gather equal parts of the following herbs:

     marjoram
     marigold
     thyme
     wormwood

     NOTE: *Wormwood is the difficult one. If you have a Chinese herbalist in your neighborhood, try there. Otherwise, do an Internet search; you can get it with a little effort.*

2. Mix the herbs together.
3. Add a little honey *(a tablespoon should do the trick)*
4. Then a bit of vinegar *(try balsamic—combined with the herbs, the aroma is pleasing).*

5. Rub the mixture on your cheeks and neck—yes, it's sticky, but so is the path to true love—as you say the following:

St. Luke, St. Luke,
Be kind to me
In dreams let me my true love see.

What you can expect:
That night, in your dreams,
you will have a vision of
your future true love.

(Sadly, there will be no hint of when girl gets boy or boy gets girl. You just get to see him or her.)

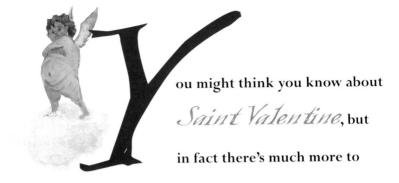

You might think you know about *Saint Valentine*, but in fact there's much more to February 14 than flowers and candy. Yes, he's still the saint to turn to if you are looking for that special man or woman. But he also has some other tricks up his sleeve.

First of all, you need to know that there isn't a real St. Valentine. Well, perhaps a better way to put it is that although there *were* several saints named Valentine—one a Persian who was stoned to death for adopting Christianity, another who was a bishop from Terni—none of them has anything to do with February 14, or love, or that little winged monstrosity…what's-its-name? Ah yes, Cupid.

The reason we call February 14 St. Valentine's Day and celebrate it with activities related to romantic love is due to the cleverness of early Christian leaders. They wanted to put the kibosh on some of the bawdier pagan festivals associated with this date, and they thought they could do so by substituting a plausible Christian substitute that would encourage more sedate behavior. *Fat chance.*

After all, February 14 had long been dubbed Lupercalia, a riotous festival sacred to Juno, the Queen of Heaven and the Roman goddess of erotic love. During this holiday, anything related to romantic love, fertility, courtship, and so on was fair game. You name it, if it had to do with boy-meets-girl *(or boy-meets-boy, or girl-meets-girl)* it happened—or was committed—under Juno's auspices. Innocent and not-so-innocent mating games were played, the most enduring being a lottery in which would-be lovers drew the names of future partners.

As Christianity spread, church officials tried to usurp February 14 as a saint's feast day—apparently hoping that thoughts of a grim and bloody death due to religious convictions might subdue some of the wilder and more carnal activities. No such luck. The partying went on, and on, and on…which is why today more than one billion Valentine's Day cards are purchased every year.

And here's an interesting fact: the evidence of there ever being a St. Valentine is so flimsy that the church removed his feast day from its official saint's calendar. Despite this, he is the only patron saint to remain on our secular calendars—a neat reversal of fortune for the mysterious Valentine.

To ask St. Valentine to intervene for you, try the following ritual. Here's a centuries-old lottery trick that worked for the lusty citizens of Rome.

Here's what you do:
1. Write the names of potential lovers on slips of paper.
2. Put the papers into a bowl *(or cup, or hat)*.
3. As you reach into the container and select one of the slips of paper, say the following:

Thou art my love and I art thine
I draw ... for my Valentine.

What you can expect:
Whosever name you choose
will be your sweetheart
by the next Valentine's Day *(February 14).*

For other rituals associated with Valentine's Day, see page 115.

riginally a simple fisherman, the *Apostle Andrew* can be invoked to see which fish you'll land.

We don't have a good explanation for why you should call on St. Andrew to glimpse your soul mate. The fisherman-turned-apostle was one of John the Baptist's followers, and he became a true believer when John proclaimed, upon seeing Jesus, "Behold the Lamb of God!" Soon Andrew and his brother Peter *(eventually the first Pope)* left their boats and nets behind to become what Jesus asked them to become, "fishers of men."

Not much is known about what Andrew did after Jesus died. Some legends say he went to Greece to preach the gospel. After that, he wandered about the civilized world preaching until he was crucified for his then-radical beliefs. Unlike Jesus, however, Andrew was tied—not nailed—to a cross. This caused his body to hang in the shape of an X—different from the way we typically envision Christ's position on the crucifix—and this X became the basis for St. Andrew's cross, which is part of the British flag today. Another version of the Andrew legend says that even while on the cross, he continued to encourage the people who had gathered around him to convert to Christianity.

To ask St. Andrew to intervene for you, try the following ritual. This ritual comes from Martin Luther himself, who recounted how German fräuleins would, on November 29, the evening before the Feast of St. Andrew *(November 30)*, strip themselves naked, and recite a prayer in order to learn what sort of husbands they would have. Consider this an equal-opportunity ritual; men as well as women can participate.

At the time, this naked exhibition was not viewed as indecent, but simply as a leftover habit of pagan worship. Many ancient peoples, Saxons in particular, seem to have made an absence of clothing part of their religious rites.

Here's what you do:

1. Find a St. Andrew's cross.

   NOTE: *If all else fails, a rendering of the British flag will do— look in your encyclopedia, go to your local British pub, or download one from the Internet.*

2. Before going to bed, take off your clothes. All of them!

   Okay, okay, if you are too modest for this, you can simply remove one item—make it your socks.

3. Recite the following prayer:

To Andrew all the lovers and the lustie wooers come
Believing, through his ayde and certain
*   ceremonies done*
To have good lucke and to obtaine
Their chiefe and sweete delight.

What you can expect:

You will dream of your future love that night.

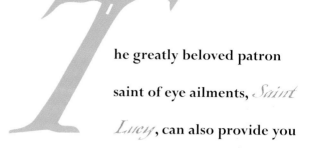

*T*he greatly beloved patron saint of eye ailments, *Saint Lucy*, can also provide you with visions of your romantic future.

Born in Sicily c. A.D. 300, Lucy, like Agnes, is another of the virgin martyrs, which means that her religious devotion and subsequent early death were tied up with her determination to remain chaste. Beautiful and high-born, she had decided early on to devote her life to performing good deeds in the name of Christ. Her pagan mother, Eutychia, wasn't convinced. A recent widow of a very rich and well-born local dignitary, Lucy's mother thought that a good *(read: wealthy)* marriage was the right thing for her daughter.

But after Lucy cured her mother of a four-year bout of painful hemorrhaging—through multiple pilgrimages and prayers to St. Agatha to intercede on her behalf—Eutychia became convinced of the rightness of Lucy's plans. She agreed to let Lucy enter a convent and devote her life to God.

Well, that's the most authentic version, based on facts known about the real Lucy's life. There are other, bloodier Lucy stories, of course—that's the way it goes with these saints. Most of these legends revolve around her rather horrifying experiences with eyes.

One version has her presenting a particularly ardent but pagan suitor with a gift of her eyes on a platter. The reason for this, er, unusual

The word elucidate, *meaning to enlighten, has the same Latin root as* Lucy.

present? He had praised her beautiful eyes, and she wanted to make it crystal clear just how important things like worldly beauty were to her. He got the message and immediately stopped with the wooing *(wouldn't you?)* in order to convert to Christianity. Lucy's eyes miraculously grew back.

Another story tells of Lucy's determination to remain true to Christ *(and celibate, of course)* despite enormous pressure from local pagan officials who wanted her to say uncle. *(Didn't these guys have anything else to do? Preside over traffic court? Round up stray dogs?)* Eventually, Lucy was hauled off to the ever-convenient local brothel, burned at the stake, and impaled on a sword. Then her eyes were plucked out. They believed in following through to the end, those pagans.

Lucy is, thus, the patron saint of eye ailments. The Swedes are particularly fond of Lucy, and they celebrate her feast day (December 13) with candles and cinnamon buns. But what about this vision-of-true-love thing? No one is quite sure, but it's a long-standing patronage, and a useful one.

To ask St. Lucy to intervene for you, try the following ritual. This is yet another ritual designed to give you a glimpse of your true love. Why so many saint-based love rituals to aid with this particular goal? We're not sure. (*But evenings must have been dull in rural medieval England. No electricity. No mall. No reruns of "The Simpsons."*)

Here's what you do:

1. Mix together 1 tablespoon each of olive oil, almond oil, and peppermint oil.
2. Before going to bed, dab a bit behind your ears, and *(carefully)* on your eyelids.
3. Place a white cloth over your eyes while you say the following:

> *Sweet Lucy let me know*
> *Whose cloth I shall lay*
> *Whose bed I shall make*
> *Whose child I should bear*
> *Whose darling I shall be*

What you can expect:

A vision of your true love, natch.

Part 2

I'm Gonna Make You Love Me

If you're ready to move beyond mere visions of love, you can get down to brass tacks with this group of saintly yentas. These heavenly matchmakers are among the most reasonably priced (and confidential) out there.

Prayers to Attract (and Keep) a Mate

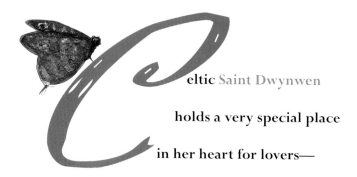

Celtic Saint Dwynwen holds a very special place in her heart for lovers—

especially if you've strayed from the straight and narrow.

Dwynwen, one of many daughters of the fifth-century Welsh king Brychan, was renowned for her goodheartedness. The Welsh even have a poem about Dwynwen's easygoing nature. A rough translation goes like this:

> *Hast thou heard the saying of St. Dwynwen*
> *The Fair daughter of Brychan the Aged?*
> *There is none so lovable or cheerful.*

Dwynwen is also known as the Welsh Venus because of her rare beauty, and her special interest in love affairs. Dwynwen was said to have blessed an ancient well in Anglesey, Ffynnon *(now destroyed)*, and for centuries it was a popular pilgrimage spot for hordes of the faithful looking to be either cured of their passion, or united with their beloved. Dwynwen would even help those who were scandalously in love with the wrong, or forbidden, person. Speaking to this, a twelfth-century scribe, Dafydd Llwyd of Mathafarn, noted with gravity that "Dwynwen will not hinder adultery," so intent is she on relieving the pangs of love from romantic sufferers.

To ask St. Dwynwen to intervene for you, try the following ritual. There is no longer a holy well in Wales devoted to Dwynwen, but we advise you to make your own, and proceed accordingly.

Here's what you do:
1. Fill a small bowl or basin with tepid water.
2. Place a small brass or gold object in the water. It should be something important to you, something that symbolizes your particular love problem—perhaps a ring, or a coin.
3. Light a candle and place it next to the bowl while saying the following prayer, a variation on a poem by medieval Welsh poet Dafydd ap Gwilym:

> *Dwynwen, in your candle-lit choir*
> *Your golden statue knows well*
> *How to soothe the pain and torment*
> *Of the lovelorn*
> *She who keeps watch in radiant holiness with you*
> *Can never depart with love-sickness nor a troubled mind.*

What you can expect:
Whatever your worry, or problem, Dwynwen will almost certainly intercede on your behalf.

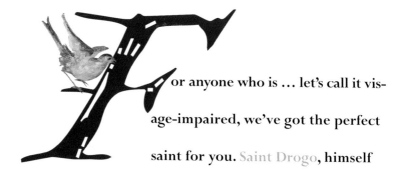

For anyone who is … let's call it vis-age-impaired, we've got the perfect saint for you. Saint Drogo, himself no beauty, makes a special effort to aid those ugly ducklings who appeal to him for help in attracting a mate.

Drogo was Flemish, born into a royal family in A.D. 800. Although he had no mother—she had died while giving birth to him—Drogo apparently lived a fairly normal life until the age of ten. At that point, some bright person decided the time was ripe to tell him that he had been the cause of his mother's death. Drogo was overcome with guilt and completely withdrew from the world. He moved into a sort of closet in the basement, and began performing extraordinary acts of physical penance—that is, whipping, burning, and starving himself in order to beg for God's forgiveness. It's hard to imagine a God that would encourage this, but Drogo apparently thought he deserved even worse. When he turned eighteen and came into his substantial inheritance *(his father had died three years previously)*, Drogo promptly gave everything away and began a series of arduous pilgrimages to Rome and other holy places. In between his journeys, and his acts of pious self-denial *(or, more accurately, self-torture)*, he humbled himself by working as a lowly shepherd in the fields of Saint Elizabeth de la Haire in Sebourg.

It was during his shepherding days that Drogo began gaining a substantial reputation as a wise and holy man. One of the miracles attributed to him is the ability to bilocate, (*that is, to be physically in two places at the same time*). Many of us would probably use this talent to catch up on our sleep while still keeping our bosses happy, but Drogo saw it as an opportunity to keep working hard at his menial job out in the pasture while simultaneously attending Mass in the village church.

Drogo settled down considerably once he found the right balance between his humble work and religious duties. But he did go on one last pilgrimage—and this is the one that gives him the patronage we're interested in. While on this journey *(no one is quite sure where he went)* he came down with a serious but unmentioned disease, perhaps leprosy, or some sort of pox. Although Drogo survived, he rose from his sickbed with a grotesquely disfigured face, and made the assessment that he was "unfit for human eyes to behold." This actually matched his inclinations nicely—and he was able to use it as an excuse to spend the last forty years of his life isolated in a hermitage, eating nothing but the Holy Eucharist from Mass, and drinking only plain well water to quench his thirst.

To ask St. Drogo to intervene for you, try the following ritual. The legend of Drogo is remarkably similar to other archetypal tales about horrifyingly ugly men who are misjudged by society despite their pure and noble hearts—such as *The Hunchback of Notre Dame*, *The Phantom of the Opera*, *The Elephant Man*, and *Beauty and the Beast*. The main difference, of course, is that Drogo—who also goes under the names of Druex, Frugo, and Druon—achieves living "happily ever after" because he is loved *(and therefore redeemed)* by God, not a beautiful girl. It is for this reason, we think, that Drogo is linked to romantic love. Don't we all hope for that special person who loves us for what's inside not out?

Here's what you do:

1. Fill a bowl with water.
2. Find a small mirror, and a bell.
3. Ring the bell three times, then dip your fingers into the water, as you say to your reflection in the mirror:

> *Drogo, you were loved*
> *Despite your lack of external beauty*
> *You had faith and courage*
> *Despite deformity*
> *Please intercede on my behalf*
> *Help me find a love*
> *Honest and true*

4. Get up at dawn the next day and say ten Paternosters *(Our Fathers)*. Do not look in a mirror again for a week.

What you can expect:

Someone who loves you for your inner beauty *will* come along. Be patient!

*I*f you find that playing insincere mind games with would-be romantic partners isn't winning you true love *(duh!)*, we recommend calling upon Saint Martin de Porres, that versatile Peruvian holy man.

St. Martin was born in the mid-1500s, the product of a racially mixed marriage in a time and place where such things were not easily tolerated. Martin's mother was a freed African slave from North America who had traveled down to Peru in search of a more hospitable homeland; his father was a Spanish nobleman who never bothered to marry Martin's mother.

Unfortunately, in sixteenth-century Peru, mixed-race children like Martin were treated as outcasts by both sides of the racial divide. Although his father refused to acknowledge him, Martin was fortunate enough to become apprenticed to a barber, and thus have a way of earning a living other than begging *(usually the only option for a man in his position)*. Martin had a talent for healing, and because barbers were also looked to as medical professionals, he soon developed a faithful following of patients who had come in for a shave and left miraculously cured of their ailments.

Although not raised in a Christian household, Martin converted at an early age, and gradually became convinced that he should devote his life to God. He took his shingle off the barbershop and knocked on the gate of the local Dominican monastery, hoping to be admitted as a member of the religious community. But even here racial discrimination raised its ugly head: the order did not accept mixed-race individuals as monks. Martin cheerfully shrugged and asked to be allowed to perform menial chores in the monastery as a way of participating in the spiritual community, albeit on the sidelines. He was paid a pittance, and slept in the stables *(performing his duties with such grace that today he is the patron saint of the poor and homeless)*.

Some remarkable powers are attributed to this gentle saint: he was reputed to be able to bilocate *(to be physically in two places at the same time)* and used this skill in order to heal twice as many people as he could otherwise have attended to. There are numerous stories about his talent for talking to animals in their own languages. This quirky hodgepodge of skills is the reason for the broad range of patronages Martin has today. We imagine it is for his compassion that he is invoked for true love. In addition, he is the protector of hairdressers and domestic animals, as well as those seeking racial and social justice.

To ask St. Martin to intervene for you, try the following ritual.

Here's what you do:

1. Get your hands on a picture or statue of St. Martin. You can find these at any standard religious shop—

St. Martin is a very popular saint.

Or try downloading one from www.catholiconline.org.

2. Turn the statue *(or picture)* upside down.

3. Place a glass of water in front of him.

4. Say the following prayer:

St. Martin
My thirst for love
Is real
As you showed compassion for those less fortunate
Help me now
In my quest for true love

5. Leave the statue upside down with the glass of water before it until your request is granted.

What you can expect:

When poor St. Martin is tired of being tormented *(by being upside down and deprived of water)* he will grant your request. Then you can return him to a more comfortable state.

NOTE: *We've always found it odd that some saint rituals— particularly those from South America—involve...well, tor- turing (or at least irritating) the saint in order to get him or her to intercede. Seems counterproductive to us. But we don't make these things up, we just report them.*

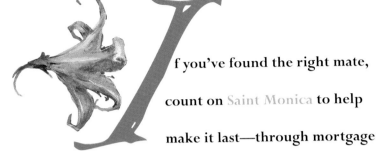

If you've found the right mate, count on Saint Monica to help make it last—through mortgage payments, colicky babies, tax audits, and other traumas that test the strength of your marriage.

Monica, the mother of St. Augustine, struggled all her life against what must have seemed a dreary conspiracy of marriage woes: addiction, adultery, and unruly children were only the half of it. It's no wonder that she is invoked when marriages are under stress.

When still a teenager, Monica was forced into a loveless marriage with a drunken, violent pagan. Her three children rebelled—first against her authority, then against society. Not only did everyone in Monica's family reject her Christianity, they seemed to go to great lengths to mock it by indulging in every carnal sin imaginable. In sorrow and depression, Monica turned to drink herself.

Eventually, Monica decided to pull her life together. First, she dried herself out. Then she managed to convince her no-good husband to join her on the wagon. By pestering him—following him to brothels, and to his mistresses' houses, and the like—she also persuaded him to settle down. Her final triumph was converting both him and his mother—the mother-in-law from hell, by all accounts—to Christianity.

Monica then started working on her dissolute children: Augustine *(soon to be the famous St. Augustine)*, Perpetua, and Navigius. They didn't have a chance. What with the wailing, and the praying, and the following from town to town, all three children eventually became Christian—Augustine with such devout passion that the rest is history. Monica's feast day is August 17, but you can appeal to her for help with your marriage on any day of the year. Like all mothers, she's always on duty.

To ask St. Monica to intervene for you, try the following ritual. Although many of the accounts of Monica's life make her seem like a candidate for the medieval equivalent of a restraining order *(she stalked her husband through the bars and brothels of all the local villages; she hounded the parish priest to pray on behalf of her womanizing, boozing children; and otherwise drove everyone who knew her to distraction)*, we choose to focus on the more thoughtful, meditative side of Monica.

Here's what you do.

1. Find a quiet, comfortable place where you won't be interrupted.

2. At dusk, sit *(or kneel)* in a comfortable position while you say the following prayer:

St. Monica
Help me find the patience, wisdom, and courage
To do what is right
For myself, and for my family

What you can expect.

The stress in your family life and marriage should ease. But, if necessary, say the prayer each night for nine consecutive nights.

This is called a novena—nine days of prayer, either public or private, dedicated to a particular saint or member of the Holy Trinity (God the Father, God the Son, or God the Holy Spirit). No set prayers are required, and it can be performed at any time.

Dear Saint Anne,

send me a man.

Need we say more?

Officially, St. Anne is the patron saint of women wanting to conceive. The reason for this is obvious: childless and well past menopause,

The term Immaculate Conception is often mistakenly believed to refer to the conception of Jesus within Mary's womb without any reproductive contribution from a human father. Actually it refers to Mary being conceived in Anne's womb without original sin. The reason for this? So that Jesus would be conceived and carried in the womb of a truly pure mother.

Anne had given up hopes of ever bearing a baby when lo and behold—she became pregnant. This baby was Mary, the mother of Jesus, and the only human after Adam and Eve's banishment from the Garden of Eden to be conceived without the stain of original sin on her infant soul.

Not much is known about Anne, although various stories abound about her desire for children, and her strong faith in God. Indeed, Anne was practically ignored until the twelfth century, when Christians around the world became more interested in Mary as a holy woman and saint in her own right *(not merely as a passive receptacle and caretaker of the infant Jesus)*. This interest spread naturally to

Mary's mother, Anne, and her worldly struggles.

Numerous folk legends relate Anne's intercessions on behalf of women for all sorts of problems. While her late-life motherhood makes her an obvious source of hope for women wanting to conceive, Anne has also been invoked for centuries by women seeking husbands.

To ask St. Anne to intervene for you, try the following ritual. The following couplet that gave this book its title is still in widespread use throughout secular America. Just ask any woman—she doesn't even need to be Catholic—between the ages of fifty and one hundred. Chances are, she'll remember this ditty.

Here's what you do:
It's easy.
Just say the following words, anytime, anyplace. Probably not on a first date, though.

Dear St. Anne
Send me a man
As quick as you can

We've also heard a slightly darker version:

Dear St Anne
Send me a man
If he lies
Or if he dies
Please, Mary's mother,
Send me another

If you're a man, try this version:

Dear Saint Nick, send me a chick

What you can expect:
A man, of course.
Although this is a minimalist
approach to matchmaking
("You want a man? We get you a man"),
it seems to work.

If you're still dating or playing the field, you can invoke Saint Raphael to ensure that all your romantic meetings are joyful ones.

Raphael, one of the seven archangels of God, can be your personal dating bodyguard, so to speak. This heavenly guardian, whose name means "God Heals," is the patron saint of happy meetings. And Raphael certainly considers romantic rendezvous his special terrain.

Raphael's particular aptitude for meetings between lovers springs from the story in the bible in the Book of Tobit in the Apocrypha, a part of the bible that generally sits at the end of the Old Testament. Raphael assumed human form to protect the long-suffering Tobit, Tobit's son Tobias, and Tobias's betrothed, Sarah. Raphael not only protected them all, but also fended off the demons that had killed Sarah's first seven husbands. *(We think Tobias was a brave man.)*

Raphael is also known as the Soldier of Health, and the Medicine of God, and is credited with easing Abraham's pain after his circumcision *(ouch)* and healing Jacob's thigh, which had been injured while wrestling with the angel.

To ask St. Raphael the Archangel to intervene for you, try the following ritual If you've ever wondered what the *arch* in *archangel* means, it's a special title awarded to a higher rank of angel than your run-of-the-mill harp-carrying variety. An *Uber-angel*, if you will. Keep that in mind, as well as the following quote, which has been attributed to Raphael, and you'll have some understanding of whom you're dealing with here:

I envy you, mortal
For you will soon see
the Glory of My Father's Heaven.
So why can you not bear your suffering
with good grace?

In other words, get back out there. It can't be *that* bad. No yenta could have said it better.

Here's what you do:

1. Find a picture of St. Raphael—these are very common, although make sure you've got Raphael, and not Gabriel *(another popular archangel)*.
2. Carry this picture with you when you venture out on your next romantic meeting. Yes, this puts the kibosh on pocketless Lycra or skintight leather *(which you shouldn't be wearing anyway)*.
3. As you approach your meeting place, say a quick prayer. Any simply worded plea will do the trick. Here's one :

Raphael, who protects as well as heals
Watch over me through this
meeting of the heart.

What you can expect:

A happy *(or at least happier)* meeting than you otherwise would have had. If your blind date stands you up, assume that Raphael was looking after you *(by making sure his Corvette got a flat tire, or her breast implants exploded, just before reaching the scheduled rendezvous point)*.

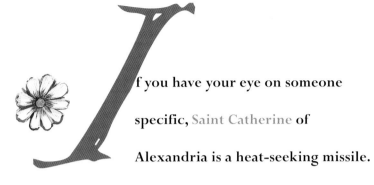

If you have your eye on someone specific, Saint Catherine of Alexandria is a heat-seeking missile.

Women have long called upon St. Catherine of Alexandria for help finding a soul mate. The reasons are clear when you look at her life story: she was very, very clear about her standards for choosing her own mate.

A fourth-century Egyptian pagan princess, Catherine was famous for her beauty and intelligence. Her father died when she was only fourteen, and when she took over the throne everyone urged her to marry—*quickly*. But Catherine had other ideas. She wouldn't marry just anyone—not the Roman emperor Maxentius *(she didn't love him)*, and not any of the other powerful and royal suitors who came calling. Indeed, Catherine was very precise about what she needed from a husband: first, she said, he must be so nobly born that everyone on earth would kneel down in worship; second, he must be so powerful in his own right that he would not feel indebted to her for making him king of Egypt; third, he must be so handsome that angels would come to earth just to look upon his face; and finally, he must be so generous and compassionate that he would forgive any and all offenses.

As you can imagine, this vastly limited Catherine's choices. Then she had a vision: Mary, the mother of Jesus, appeared to her in a dream and suggested her son as a suitable bridegroom. Just as Catherine was mulling this over, Christ made it clear that *he* rejected *her*, adding insult to injury by saying that Catherine "was not beautiful enough." This shook our Catherine up enough to convert to Christianity—and Mary promptly reappeared with Jesus, who accepted Catherine as his spiritual bride. When Catherine woke up from the vision, she was wearing a wedding ring, the only problem being that it was invisible to everyone but her. (*Naturally, this gave her a bit of a credibility problem.*)

The emperor Maxentius, still smarting from getting his walking papers, asked Catherine to undergo a trial that tested her newly forged faith by setting up a debate between her and fifty pagan philosophers. After Catherine converted every single one, Maxentius killed them and gave Catherine one more chance to marry him. At her refusal, Maxentius had her beaten and tied to a torture wheel *(thereafter called a Catherine's Wheel)*. But don't underestimate Catherine—first she converted the hundreds of soldiers who were guarding her, then an angel appeared and destroyed the wheel. Maxentius, just about at the end of his sadistic rope by this point, ordered his soldiers to behead Catherine. When the dirty deed was done, milk rather than blood flowed from Catherine's neck, and a flock of singing angels descended from heaven to take

Catherine's body *(and head, one assumes)* to Mount Sinai for burial.

After her death, Catherine was made a doctor of the Catholic Church—the highest academic honor, and one not often bestowed on women—because of the vast and deep theological knowledge she exhibited during her trials.

To ask St. Catherine to intervene for you, try the following ritual. Because of the pickiness she displayed in selecting a mate, Catherine is the patron saint for women seeking not just husbands, but great husbands. A number of whimsical medieval rhymes survive that attest to her popularity in this role.

Here's what you do: Simply say one of the following prayers, as often as you like:

A husband, St. Catherine,
A good one, St. Catherine,
A handsome one, St. Catherine,
A rich one, St. Catherine,
And soon, St. Catherine!

or

Sweet St. Catherine, send me a husband,
A good one, I pray,
But anyone better than none.
Oh St. Catherine, lend me thine aid,
That I may not die an old maid.

What you can expect:
Nothing less than the *crème de la crème* of husbands.

There's also another ritual with a slight twist:
It's for women who are seeking relief from bad marriages.

Here's what you do:
Fast *(don't eat anything, and drink only water)* every
Wednesday and every Saturday for an entire year,
and make sure not to eat on St. Catherine's feast day
(November 25), either.

What you can expect:
If you manage to do the fasting without missing a single
day—even if you are ill—Catherine will come to your aid.
What does this mean? We're not sure. We don't know anyone
who has successfully completed it. Furthermore, we certainly
don't advocate starving yourself two days out of seven for any
extended period of time. Maybe biweekly couples-counseling
sessions are a better way to go.

There's a strange little addendum to this particular ritual. Married women won't necessarily see their marriages improve—they'll just be relieved of the "burden" of an unhappy marriage. Your marriage may in fact *end*—through "death or desertion," as one source puts it. Seems a poor, or even evil, object for prayer, but then medieval women didn't have divorce court to remedy truly impossible domestic situations.

Part 3

Calling All Saintly Dear Abbys

The course of true love never did run smooth, and here's proof: even the saints have been called in over the ages to help with this most mysterious of human conditions. So move over Oprah,, Abby, and Ann. You are rank amateurs compared to the saintly lineup found in this section.

Heavenly Help for the Lovelorn, Loveless, or (Even) Overloved

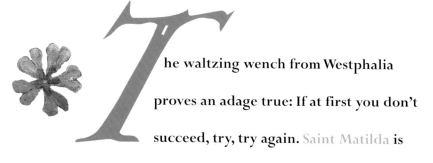

The waltzing wench from Westphalia proves an adage true: If at first you don't succeed, try, try again. Saint Matilda is the patron saint of second marriages.

Nearly half of all American marriages end in divorce. Luckily, despite the Catholic Church's long-standing disapproval of men *(and women)* rending what God hath joined together, we're happy to say you can still find church-sanctioned solace of sorts if your first, second, or even third marriage has been a bust. *(It's not that we're pro-divorce—that's like being pro-liver-transplant—it's that we're anti-living-in-hell-on-earth.)*

The woman for the formidable job of marriage-rescue is Matilda, born around A.D. 895, who made a successful marriage, at least according to the snobbish standards of her noble parents. Matilda's father was Count Deitrich of Westphalia, her mother Countess Reinheld of Denmark, and they had long planned for their only daughter to marry a coarse and ambitious German nobleman named Henry the Fowler of Saxony, whose first marriage had ended in divorce.

Things got dicey very quickly. Almost as soon as Matilda was getting used to being married to a total stranger, a bizarre series of political coincidences caused her uncouth husband Henry to be crowned king of Germany. He was overjoyed, of course. But poor Matilda! She was ill-suited to being a queen. She loathed the power and wealth that were suddenly in her hands, and rather than reveling in her new position, embarked on a strategy of quietly devoting herself to God without openly declaring her position. Rarely seen at court, Matilda spent most of her time in meditation and prayer at remote convents. Her only public appearances were related to her charitable efforts. Matilda poured money and time into works that aided the poor, sick, and downtrodden within her husband's kingdom.

Meanwhile, everyone had expected Matilda's husband, Henry, a coarse lout from the backwoods of Bavaria, to grow even more corrupt and dissolute in his position of power. But the opposite occurred. Henry fell in love with his wife's gentle ways. Eventually she decided that the change was for real and grew to love him in return, taming his wildness and converting him to a wholehearted acceptance of God.

Henry supported Matilda's unusual habits —her preference for the company of ragged wretches over upscale members of court, her fondness for founding Benedictine abbeys in mountain crevices, and her tendency to hand over the royal riches to the poor as fast as she could unload them from the treasury vaults. They remained a devoted and passionate duo until his sudden death in 936.

At Henry's funeral Mass, Matilda appeared in an extravagant bridal gown encrusted with precious stones and jewels. She declared that her goal was to get married again, and as quickly as possible—but this time, of course, her bridegroom would be Christ. As she completed her vows, Matilda dramatically stripped off her finery, giving the fortune in jewels that she was wearing to the priest and bidding him to distribute it among the poor.

We are almost at "happily ever after" here, but our heroine had one more hurdle to face. Matilda appointed her son, Henry Jr. *(also known as Henry the Quarrelsome)*, to succeed her husband as king of Germany. Another son, Otto, had been coveting the job and decided to ignite a scandal by accusing his mother of mismanaging the royal money. *(Well, we suppose if giving it away was "mismanaging," Matilda was guilty as charged.)* Already unpopular with the royals because of her sympathy for the poor, Matilda was told she was no longer welcome at court—something that probably made her break out the Dom Perignon and put on her dancing shoes for one last whoopee. She happily trotted off to a remote mountain convent and spent the last thirty-two years of her life in solitude, devoting herself to prayer and penance. She died peacefully in 968 and was buried alongside her true love, her husband.

The most obvious reason for Matilda to be the patron of second marriages is that she succeeded in building a happy marriage between herself and a man who had been married before. We'd also like to point out that she remained open and generous and full of compassion even when things weren't working out the way she'd thought or hoped they would.

Matilda is also the patron saint of children who disappoint, the falsely accused, and unwilling queens. *(We're sure there's an off-Broadway musical buried in this material, but that's another project.)*

To ask St. Matilda to intervene for you, try the following ritual.

Here's what you do:

1. Buy a white rose, or pick one from your garden.

   NOTE: The operative words are: *buy* and *your garden*.
   There's no payoff for unscrupulous flower thieves.

2. Scatter the petals on your pillowcase.
3. Before going to sleep, say the following prayer:

   St. Matilda,
   A happy marriage you did see
   With a man who married another before ye
   Guide my steps, my heart, my fate
   As you bring to me another mate
   All true marriage does entail
   Open heart, true soul, and blessed detail

4. Say the same prayer as soon as you awake in the morning.
5. Sometime that day—before the sun sets—make a contribution to the charity of your choice. *(If you're low on funds, why not go through your wardrobe and give all your when-I-get-back-in-shape clothes to Goodwill? Many birds are killed with this stone—ritual fulfilled, closet cleaned, catalyst for feeling guilty about all those pints of Chunky Monkey removed.)*

What you can expect:
Love will be better the second time around.

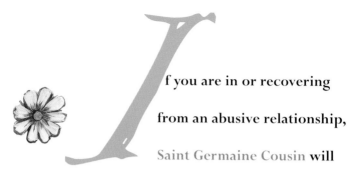

If you are in or recovering

from an abusive relationship,

Saint Germaine Cousin **will**

provide balm for your body and soul.

This humble farm girl was born in the late 1500s and lost her mother before she could walk. She then suffered through one crippling illness after another throughout her miserable childhood. Her chronic health problems resulted in a number of permanent deformities and disabilities—one of her hands was withered and unusable, her face was pock-marked, and her body was covered with painful oozing sores.

Her father had quickly remarried after his wife's death, and as in the fairy tales, this turned out to be bad news for poor little Germaine. She was kicked out of the house and forced to sleep in the stable with the animals; left to starve, she scavenged what she could from the leftovers put out for the dogs. Her stepmother and increasing brood of stepbrothers and stepsisters took great pleasure in physically abusing her. Worse, they told her she deserved it because she was so sinful. Germaine never became bitter though. Instead she thanked God for what she had, and even gave away the few comforts she possessed to other local children who were abused or neglected.

At nine years old, Germaine was sent out to the fields to work as a shepherdess for the local landowner. Although her family confiscated her meager salary, Germaine was happy because the relative autonomy and solitude of the work allowed her plenty of time to pray and say her rosary. She loved to gather the village children about her in order to teach them about Jesus. Gradually word spread that she was performing miracles: angels minded Germaine's flock so she could go to Mass; she walked across a raging river in order to get to church on time; and she never lost a sheep to illness or predators. But although her reputation grew among the townsfolk, Germaine was still treated poorly by her own family.

One day Germaine's stepmother caught her in the family larder, her apron obviously full of something. When accused of stealing food to give to the poor, Germaine promptly opened her apron. But instead of any ill-gotten goods, an array of exotic flowers fell to the floor. Her evil stepmother was impressed despite herself—after all, it was January, and the snow was more than five feet deep. Worried that Germaine might be a more important person than they had previously thought, her family invited her to rejoin them. Germaine refused, saying she preferred to continue her simple existence. Germaine died in the early 1600s, apparently of natural causes: she was found one morning curled up on her straw pallet, lifeless. The townspeople convinced the local priest to give her an honored burial spot in the churchyard. Some twenty

Just emerging from a bad marriage or long-term relationship? Saint Helena can be counted on to help the newly single mingle.

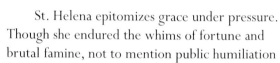

St. Helena epitomizes grace under pressure. Though she endured the whims of fortune and brutal famine, not to mention public humiliation by her ex, St. Helena never lost her generous spirit—or her faith.

At first Helena's marriage to Constantius Chlorus, co-regent of the western Roman empire *(sort of like an up-and-coming VP of sales for a successful but not spectacular business)* seemed a happy one. Then their first child was born. This baby, a son, was destined to become Constantine the Great, although of course no one knew this at the time *(kind of like a baby Bill Gates before anyone had even heard of a PC)*.

The new baby put a strain on the marriage. Constantius Senior lost it: he slept with prostitutes, he slept with his wife's best friends, he probably slept with the thirteenth century's equivalent of the babysitter. After all this, Constantius dumped Helena so he could marry another woman with strong political clout in Rome *(a Byzantine version of a trophy wife)*.

Helena bore her betrayal and subsequent banishment with good grace. She retreated with dignity to an outpost of the Roman Empire, and for the next several years raised her son to possess all the noble qualities his father lacked. This son, well on his way to earning his celebrated moniker, established his mother at court with power and wealth as soon as he was crowned emperor *(no word on what revenge he wreaked on his father)*.

Once at court, Helena exploded with good deeds. She used her high position and new wealth to build dozens of Christian missions and magnificent cathedrals and churches. These can still be visited throughout southern France. At the ripe old age of eighty she led a group of pilgrims to the Holy Land to look for the original cross on which Jesus had been crucified. They found a cross, and it was proved to be authentic when a woman dying of an incurable disease was miraculously cured by touching it. Helena proceeded to build a church on the spot. This is why she is usually depicted in art carrying a wooden cross.

To ask St. Helena to intervene for you, try the following ritual.

Here's what you do.

1. Construct a simple cross out of paper or cardboard. Decorate it as much as you like *(nothing extreme needed— but keep in mind that Helena delighted in commissioning beautiful cathedrals in God's name)*.

2. Hang the cross near a window that lets in direct sunlight.

3. For nine days straight, say the following prayer:

(This is called a novena—see page 42)

Helena, help me attain some portion
Of your calm acceptance,
Your steadfast faith
In the face of betrayal and pain.
Guide me through this rugged
*   emotional terrain,*
Allow me to emerge with my soul
*   and ability to love intact.*

What you can expect:
Some reduction of the pain
of an unhappy or faithless relationship.
You will love again.

*I*f you are currently separated from your

spouse, but making a genuine effort to

reconcile, Saint Edward the Confessor

might be the right saint to ask for help.

 Edward was the son of King Ethelred III and his Norman wife, Emma, who lived in the early sixth century. The family dynamics are way too complicated to elaborate on here, but suffice it to say that the Ethelred clan had long ago taken up permanent residence at Dysfunction Junction.

Young Edward earned the nickname "the Confessor" because of the extreme piety and spiritual fervor he displayed from an early age. Despite his angelic appearance *(and general deportment)*, Eddie insisted to everyone that he was really a bad, bad boy who needed to be punished. He especially delighted in going to church and confessing his supposedly many sins, hence the nickname that was coined before he was out of diapers. After his father died, Edward embarked on a frenzy of social and political reform, and was apparently quite ahead of his time in calling for tax refunds and campaign finance reform.

It's a bit unclear why Edward is invoked on behalf of separated couples, but perhaps his exceedingly odd marriage has something to do with it. Edward was engaged at an early age to the daughter of one of his tutors. He loved and respected Edith, but apparently it was the love of a brother for a sister. Being an honorable man, Edward fulfilled the engagement and married Edith, but—exceedingly hard luck for her— told her it would by necessity be a celibate marriage. Edward never wavered on this point throughout their long married life. Okay, so he had certain… issues.

To ask St. Edward to intervene for you, try the following ritual:

Here's what you do:
1. Pick three red flowers and three yellow ones and place them in a glass full of water.
2. Write, or "confess" your fears, hopes, and dreams on slips of paper. Add them to the glass.
3. Say a novena *(see page 42)* for the next nine days.

What you can expect:
The best outcome, whatever that may be. Edward is a powerful ally.

*I*f you feel crowded by an unwanted admirer,

Saint Wilgefortis is your man—er, woman.

Wilgefortis has a number of aliases—

St. Uncumber and St. Liberata, among others.

An odd duck, Wilgefortis is still one of the most practical saints to have on your side when "no" doesn't seem to register with an overardent suitor. Think of her as your spiritual restraining order.

Wilgefortis was one of the many daughters *(all newly converted Christians)* of the fourteenth century pagan king of Portugal. Wilgefortis knew from an early age that her lot as a royal daughter was to be married off to a political ally of her father's, and a pagan no less *(she had seen it happen to each of her five older sisters)*.

Wilgefortis vowed not to let her sisters' fate become hers. So when her father told her she was scheduled to be married to the king of Sicily, a neighboring pagan buddy of his, Wilgefortis calmly informed him that she had taken a vow of celibacy. *(These virgin martyrs didn't have as much fun defending their faith as, say, St. Benedict, or St. Anthony, who at least got to travel and see the world. But they understood and exploited the sole source of power they possessed.)*

Her father ignored Wilgefortis's vow and subsequent objections to getting hitched. And here is where she distinguishes herself from the other virgin martyrs. There would be no gouging out of eyes or burning at the stake for this strong-willed early feminist. Instead, Wilgefortis hit upon the mischievous notion of asking God to make her too unattractive for any man to desire. God must have been amused at this unusual request, because Wilgefortis promptly grew a beard and mustache. When word got back to the king of Sicily, he quickly rescinded his offer, and since no other candidates appeared, Wilgefortis got to keep her virtue as well as her facial hair, and lived out her days praying and fasting and devoting herself to God.

The cult of St. Wilgefortis first came to the notice of the church soon after her death, when priests became aware that women in their parishes were praying to an obscure and sexually ambiguous saint to help them get rid of unwanted husbands. Despite attempts by the church to discourage this "nonsense," the cult of Wilgefortis spread like wildfire as women across Europe built shrines and prayed for her to intercede on their behalf. At some point *(no one is quite sure when this happened)*, women began offering oats to St. Wilgefortis when visiting her shrine. After requesting that she bless them, the women took the oats back home and fed them to their husband's horses. *(The idea was that the spiritually superpowered oats would allow the horse to swiftly take the offending husband away.)*

Today, scholars believe that the Wilgefortis legend sprung from a crucifix found in a small church in Lucca, Italy. Lucca was a popular stop for medieval pilgrimages, and pilgrims marveled at the long gown and the bejeweled head of the Christ figure on this crucifix—a very womanly figure despite the obvious presence of a beard and mustache. Scholars now say it may have been the sexual ambiguity of this widely viewed image that sparked the legend of the bearded lady saint.

Church officials were not pleased with this particular saint's cult. Among other critics, Sir Thomas More condemned the practice of using prayer to get rid of a husband as "despicable." She was removed from the official church calendar of saints in 1969. Yet Wilgefortis's power endures among women who need help coping with unreasonable spouses. You can still find Mass cards with her image on them, and her cult is active among women in rural parts of eastern Europe. And frankly, we think she's a good resource for men, too—no one should have to bear the attentions of an avid and unwanted lover.

To ask St. Wilgefortis to intervene for you, try the following ritual.

Here's what you do:

1. Light a candle *(any simple votive will do)*.
2. Surround it with oats *(Cheerios, plain or Honey-Nut)*.
3. Say the following prayer:

> *St. Wilgefortis, please take away this bothersome suitor*
>
> [Name him or her]
>
> *Unencumber me from his/her unwanted affections Liberate me from any obligations to respond*

What you can expect:

Your bothersome suitor should get the hint.

When you are utterly without hope, lovely Saint Rita will be there to pick up the pieces of your shattered heart.

Rita can be invoked for all sorts of hopeless causes, but especially those relating to love, and especially the love woes of women. Why Rita? Mostly because she has been there and done that to a degree that would have exhausted most of us. We like to think of her as a feminine counterpart to St. Jude *(your patron for impossible situations)*: Jude is always appropriate, but when you need that womanly touch, we recommend Rita.

Rita Lotti was born in 1381 in Roccaporena, Italy, a tiny hamlet located near Cascia, in the province of Umbria. Her parents were extremely pious—and very, very old. For this reason they were concerned about their only daughter's future. While Rita longed to enter religious life, her parents worried about the intrigue and political instability that permeated even the most supposedly unworldly convents, and instead wanted her to be married young and married well.

A dutiful daughter, Rita did her parents' bidding and married Paolo Mancini, the town watchman—a sort of medieval police officer. After twin sons were born, Rita devoted her life to keeping the home fires burning—that is, until Paolo was murdered by the medieval equivalent of organized crime who opposed the current governors of the town. *(Paolo, as a sort of civil servant, was more or less in the camp of the government.)* Poor Rita had barely become accustomed to being a widow when she lost both her sons to illness. For solace, she turned to God, devoting herself to prayer and charitable works. Eventually, she revived her hope of joining a religious order. But despite her obvious piety, she was refused entry into the Augustinian nuns of Cascia not once, not twice, but three times. Apparently, her husband's political affiliations and the violent nature of his death worried church officials.

Rita didn't take this news lying down. She kneeled. And prayed, and fasted—and got to work reconciling the rival factions in town so that everyone could live in peace. Once this was achieved, she was admitted into the convent and devoted the next forty years of her life to prayer and service to the poor.

One last note about this long-suffering woman: as she knelt in prayer one morning in the chapel, Rita felt something sharp piercing her head. It was a thorn—much like the thorns on the "crown" Jesus was made to wear as he carried the cross through the streets of Jerusalem. No one could remove the thorn from Rita's head, and so she lived with the pain *(but also, one assumes, the glory)* of this mystical thorn for the next fifteen years, until her death. Because of this, Rita is frequently depicted in art with a bloody thorn embedded in her forehead, holding a skull, a crucifix, or both.

There's no direct link between Rita and women who are seeking love—after all, Rita never sought it herself, and in fact was able to achieve her heart's desire only after her marriage ended. But she is clearly capable of solving seemingly impossible situations, so perhaps she should be reserved for only your thorniest romantic cases.

To ask St. Rita to intervene for you, try the following ritual.

Here's what you do:

1. Somehow get your hands on a thorn—try a rose bush, a cactus, or other thorny plant. *(Do not put it in your forehead. No extra points for crazy stuff.)*

2. Also find a picture of St. Rita. You can find medals with her image at most religious supply stores *(she's very popular—up there with Christopher and Jude).*

3. Place the thorn in front of the picture of St. Rita while saying the following:

St. Rita
Who endured, persevered, and
Remained faithful throughout long trials
Help me to remain steadfast and
loyal to my quest for love

What you can expect:
Balm for your broken heart.

Yes, Virginia, there is a Saint Gomer, and he is invoked for lovers in difficult relation-ships *(and for help with naughty spouses).*

Born around A.D. 717, Gomer was a soldier as well as a saint who lived until what was then the ripe old age of sixty in what would now be called Germany, but which was then part of the Roman Empire.

A brave and valiant fighter, Gomer served in the Roman army under Pepin the Short through year after year of bloody battles. *(Our big question here is: Who was Pepin the Short, and how did his subjects keep themselves from giggling when addressing him?)* Coincidentally, several other saints who served under Pepin the Short are also invoked by those in bad marriages.

Not to stray from the hero of our story, Gomer. Although born into a rich and influential family, Gomer was variously described as pious, innocent, and simple by those who knew him. Town gossips also noted that he liked to spend time with wise old men rather than pretty young girls. To each his own, we would say today, but this being medieval times, Gomer was "encouraged" to marry a young woman named Gwinmarie. You can guess who did the encouraging: yes, Pepin the Peewee himself.

Gwinmarie was an early version of a pop princess: rich, beautiful, and hip. Contrary to what you might expect, at first she was besotted with Gomer; he was so different from the crude slackers who chose to hang around the taverns of Bavaria rather than march off to war. Dear Reader, she married him! But before they could even begin to get acquainted, Pepin needed Gomer back on the battlefield.

After mourning the departure of her new groom, Gwinmarie took over the running of the estate, and apparently was so talented that when Gomer returned there was little for him to do but relate war stories to anyone who would listen. *("Hey! Did I tell you about the time I was lost in the cistern?")* Soon bored by domestic life, Gomer left to fight more barbarians in Lombardy, Saxony, and Aquitaine. He returned home less and less frequently as it became clear that this marriage had not been made anywhere near heaven.

In Gomer's absence, Gwinmarie evolved into a powerful political presence. Eventually she was running the town and bullying neighbors and local merchants to the point that Gomer was increasingly called home to settle disputes before blood was shed. As quickly as possible, though, Gomer would be off again. And when he was home, he'd go on pilgrimages with friends in an attempt to avoid his increasingly belligerent wife.

It was on one of these so-called pilgrimages that Gomer saw an angel descend into his bedchamber one night. The angel told Gomer, in no uncertain terms, that he needed to turn around at once, go home, and build a monastery and a church on his estate. Gomer did as instructed.

After Gomer built the monastery, we run into one of those baffling gaps so common in the biographies of the early saints. All we know for sure is that for the rest of his life Gomer remained at home, still married to Gwinmarie, but in name only. He went his way *(in meditation and prayer)*, and she went hers *(back to bullying, we guess)*.

Years later, on Gwinmarie's deathbed, she and Gomer reconciled. Just minutes after his not-quite-beloved wife, Gomer also died. Bizarrely, they were survived by a large brood of children, all of whom must have been miraculously conceived *(as far anyone knew their marriage had never been consummated—no wonder Gwinmarie was so belligerent)*. Though we're not entirely sure, this last ditch reconciliation must be the reason that thus Gomer became a patron for troubled marriages.

To ask St. Gomer to intervene for you, try the following ritual.

Here's what you do:

1. Get thee to a garden.
2. Dig thee a patch of earth to prepare for planting.
3. Plant four separate saplings, flowers, or bushes— make sure they are perennials, not annuals.
4. When done, say the following prayer.

> *St. Gomer*
> *Who understood the agony of a bad marriage*
> *Let me grow tall and supple*
> *And flourish ever stronger*
> *Year after year*
> *Always hoping for eternal spring*

What you can expect:

Frankly, the moral of the tale of Gomer baffles us. However, if all else fails, we recommend trying to build a monastery on your "estate."

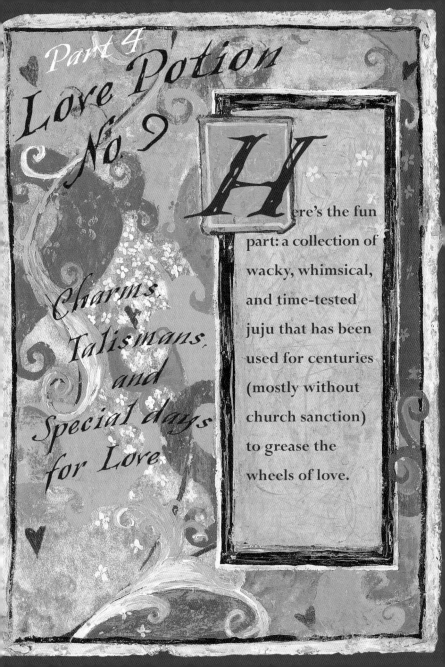

Part 4

Love Potion No 9

Charms, Talismans, and Special days for Love

Here's the fun part: a collection of wacky, whimsical, and time-tested juju that has been used for centuries (mostly without church sanction) to grease the wheels of love.

Dumb Cake

MANY OF THE SAINT-BASED LOVE RITUALS THAT COME
to us from medieval England require you to bake *(and often eat)* a rather
tasteless pastry that is commonly referred to as a dumb cake.

This cake gets its name from the fact that it must be made in
silence. Often, the success of the ritual depends on this silence
remaining unbroken for an extended period of time—until dawn,
for example. And some rituals specify that the dumb cake be made
at a precise time—usually after dark, sometimes at the stroke of
midnight—or the potency of the love charm will be affected.

The dumb cake recipe varies depending on the ritual, but it tends
to be simple, involving little more than mixing eggs, flour, salt, and water
together in slightly varying proportions. The more challenging aspect is
the silence. For although you can certainly make one by yourself, most of
the traditional love rituals involve two, three, or even more participants.
We think this was a medieval attempt at mischief—the more of you there
are in the kitchen a-mixing and a-baking, and probably a-tippling, the
greater the chance for interesting late-night secret-telling.

Please note that although in the past dumb cakes were exclusively
the province of women, we think that in these enlightened times they
should be equal-opportunity pastries. Men, start your ovens.

Here are some rituals to try: One of the most common
reasons to bake a dumb cake is to get a glimpse of a future
spouse. And there are specific days that traditionally have been
reserved for this kind of ritual, as follows.

All Saints Eve, or Halloween: Traditionally Halloween is one of the most magical nights of the year for divining the future, and dumb cake is essential to many related pagan rituals. Church officials attempted but failed to get early Christians to transfer their various spiritual practices from pagan deities to Christian saints on this particular night—on which, it was believed, the boundaries between the spirit and material worlds were weakest. Unlike other pagan-turned-Christian dates *(like Christmas and Easter)*, we still tend to think of October 31 in strictly secular terms. *(See page 120 for more.)*

If you decide to make a dumb cake on Halloween, you won't be able to ask for a private unveiling of your future mate: the ritual requires at least three participants before any results will be delivered.

Here's what you do:

1. In silence, combine the following ingredients:

   1 egg
   1 eggshellful of salt
   1 eggshellful of wheat flour
   1 eggshellful of barley flour
   1 eggshellful of rainwater *(just use bottled spring water unless you are very patient)*

2. Mix together thoroughly. And—this is important!—each person participating must take a turn stirring the mixture.

3. When you have something that resembles a flat slab of sticky dough, each lovelorn supplicant marks his or her initials somewhere on its surface.

4. Bake for 20 minutes at 350 degrees.

(That's our guess—the traditional instructions are no help, as they simply instruct you to place the cake "near the fire" until done.)

Remember, no talking! Also, no one is allowed to leave the kitchen between the time that the preparation of the dumb cake begins and the baked cake is removed from the oven, or the charm won't work.

There are a number of different versions of the Halloween dumb cake ritual. Some of them instruct the participants to stay as far away from the fire *(oven)* as possible. Some are even more restrictive, requiring that the cake be made between 11 P.M. and midnight, for example, or stipulating that each participant must turn the baking cake over at least once.

What you can expect:

After the clock strikes midnight, the first person to be married will have a vision of his or her future spouse. *(We're a little unclear on the particulars here. Will the other participants be permitted a glimpse of this vision, or does it appear only to the chosen one? How will the vision manifest itself? Would it appear like the face of Abraham Lincoln in the water stain on the ceiling of a cheap motel? What happens if one of the participants is destined to have a whole string of future husbands and wives? Does it ever get ugly in the kitchen if rival-future-spouse visions collide? Your guess is as good as ours.)*

The only other direction we found said that this apparition might choose to place a ghostly hand over the initials on the cake made by the person who is destined to be his or her spouse. *Scary!*

We hazard a guess that there might have been some tippling of mead or blackberry wine in medieval kitchens to help this vision thing along. But that's just modern cynicism rearing its ugly head. Try it yourself to find out.

St. Faith's Eve *(January 21)*: This version of the dumb cake ritual is almost identical to the one to be performed on Halloween, with the following minor differences:

1. The cake must be turned over three times while baking by each person participating. *(No big deal. Just take turns with the spatula.)*
2. After taking the cake out of the oven and allowing it to cool for 10 minutes, you must cut the cake into long thin strips *(as thin as possible without causing the cake to crumble).* Make sure you have enough strips to go around.
3. Each person participating in the ritual must pass one strip of cake three times through a wedding ring borrowed from a woman or man who has been happily married for at least seven years. *(There are two challenges here: first, to convince someone to lend his or her ring to you and your cohorts, who, frankly, may appear to be a bunch of nuts; and also to somehow verify that the marriage in question is truly happy. Go ahead, get the skinny.)* All of this must be done in absolute silence.
4. After the pass-through-the-wedding-ring stuff is done, each person says the following prayer while eating his or her share of the dumb cake. *(This talking-with-the-*

mouth-full instruction is gross, but perhaps you can look away from your collaborators at this point.) Obviously, you no longer need to remain silent after this stage of the proceedings.

> *O good St. Faith, be kind tonight*
> *And bring to me my heart's delight*
> *Let me my future husband/wife view*
> *And be my vision chaste and true*

What you can expect.

A vision, we hope not an alarming one.

Again, there's no direction on where this eerie vision will appear. On the television? Your watch? We suspect this might have been a medieval version of spin the bottle. You'll be left gazing—surprise!—at your cohorts' faces.

St. Mark's Eve *(April 24)*: Bake the dumb cake before midnight. You can use the All Saint's Eve recipe on page 82, or—since this is one of the few rituals that require you to actually eat the cake—you might want to spice it up a bit. Among other things unique to this version:

1. Precisely three people must participate—no more, no less.
2. As soon as the clock strikes midnight, each person must break off a piece of the cake to eat. The entire cake must be consumed for the ritual to work *(another reason to go with an enhanced recipe or packaged cake mix)*.

3. And here comes the hard part: while eating the cake, you have to *walk to bed backwards*. That's right—backwards. Oh, and no speaking, or the spell is broken. *(We don't know what the effect is of tripping over the ottoman, or stepping on the dog's paw.)*

What you can expect.

If you are destined to get married, you will dream of your future spouse(s) that night.

A footnote to this ritual informs us that if you hear any unusual noises during the night—any creaking or knocking or other strange nocturnal sounds—you can rest assured that your marriage will be a happy one. If you are destined never to marry, you will not hear any such noises, and to make the bad news go down with a pinch of rat poisoning, you'll also have horrible dreams of death.

One last version.

There is a silent *(dumb)* but cakeless ritual to be performed on St. Mark's Eve *(April 24)* that requires you to eat the raw yolk of an egg in silence, then fill the shell with salt and place it on a windowsill in your bedroom. If you are going to be married, you will have a vision of your future spouse that night. *You'll probably also get really sick.*

Egg Charms

THE TRADITION OF COLORING EASTER eggs, and giving egg-shaped gifts in the spring—today, we prefer chocolate!—goes way back, to long before the celebration of Easter. In pagan times eggs represented the rebirth of nature after winter—the time when flowers bloomed, animals came out of hibernation, and farmers could begin preparing for the growing season. Not surprisingly, eggs were thought to have special magical powers, particularly in matters of fertility and love, and the divination of matters pertaining to these concerns. After the death of Jesus, Christians turned the egg into a symbol of Christ's resurrection, but some religious scholars even believe that the word *Easter* comes from pagans—the name of the goddess of spring was Oestar.

Today, eggs remain an essential part of folk rituals involving fertility, marriage, and love. Below are some love-related egg rituals you might want to try. Unlike many other rituals, these can be performed at any time of the year—no special days are designated as more conducive to success than others.

Here are some rituals to try:

There are a number of rituals that use placing an egg white in a glass of water to determine the occupation of your future mate. *(As usual, this was traditionally a woman's ritual. But today, it's just as much in the man's interest to find out the earnings potential of his future wife.)* One version of this ritual is as follows.

Here's what you do:

1. Break a whole egg into a bowl of water placed in direct sunlight.
2. Leave the egg in the sun for at least 5 minutes.

What you can expect:

When the white floats to the top, the shape of the goo should resemble the vocation of your future mate.

(We don't suggest you do this before a blind date; you'll be jumpy enough without seeing your dinner partner as an egg the rest of the night.)

Here's an egg-related ritual for your wedding day,

(an alternative to the standard carry-over-the-threshold thing):

Here's what you do:

1. Crush an egg with your foot as you step through the door of your first matrimonial home.

   (But tell your new spouse about it first. Insanity can still be used as grounds for divorce.)

What you can expect:

A happy marriage.

NOTE: If you're currently in a relationship, and you want to stay in it, never *ever* bring eggs into your house after dark. This causes such devastating luck that you may as well begin packing immediately.

Apple Charms

THIS FRUIT WAS USED IN PAGAN RITUALS IN A range of creative ways—primarily in divination, and by people searching for love. As with many formerly pagan rituals, over the centuries the efficacy of these apple charms was half-heartedly attributed to the intervention of one Christian saint or another, although there was rarely a logical connection.

Here are some rituals to try:

St. Simon and St. Jude, who share October 28 as their feast day, are often appealed to with apple charms. We have no idea why, since both were fishermen and have patronages for water-related professions—nor do we know how these two became associated with romance. Regardless, there is an apple ritual associated with these two that you can perform in order to discover the identity of future loves.

Here's what you do:

1. Pare the skin off an apple, taking care to keep the skin in one piece. *(That is, instead of cutting off pieces of apple skin, make one continuous cut. The peel will be long and curling as a result.)*

2. Take the peel in your right hand. Standing in the middle of the room, say the following:

> *Saints Simon and Jude, on you I intrude*
> *By this parting I hold to discover,*
> *Without any delay, to tell me this day*
> *The first letter of my own true lover*

3. Turn three times around, and
   cast the peel over your left shoulder.

What you can expect:
When the peel lands, it will form the first letter of your future lover's last name. *(We especially suggest this ritual if you have a crush on someone whose last name begins with C, O, or U.)* If the peel breaks, or falls flat so that no letter is discernible, you will never marry. *(We'd like to soften that one by saying maybe you'll never marry someone with a last name. Think Braveheart. Fabio. Madonna. Cher.)*

After you have performed the ritual, you should take the seeds of the same apple, put them into spring water, and drink them in order to make the prediction come true.

All Saints Eve, or **Halloween**: October 31 is a prime time for playing with apple charms. Even today, a popular Halloween party game is "bobbing for apples," although the original point of the game— to catch a glimpse of the future—has been lost. *(Traditionally, you could determine everything from your future profession, to your expected death date—!—to, naturally, the identity of a future lover by playing this game.)*

Most Halloween apple rituals involve the pips, or seeds, of an apple, and they also frequently require a fire, although perhaps a lit gas stove burner might do the trick.

Here's what you do:

1. First, fix your mind on the person you love—or one you'd like to date—and, addressing him or her silently, throw an apple seed into the fire while saying:

If you love me
Pop and fly
If you hate me
Lay and die

What you can expect:
If the pip bursts from the heat and makes a substantial noise, you are loved; if it simply burns silently, you should give up hope of having a satisfactory relationship with the person in question.

Torn between two lovers? Here's another All Saints Eve apple trick.

Here's what you do:

1. Take two apple seeds, and press one on each of your cheeks as you name the two men or women *(or whatever combination fits your lifestyle)* who are battling for your affections.
2. Say the following with the seeds stuck to your cheeks:

See from the core two kernels brown I take
This on my cheek for Lubberkin is worn

And Boobyclod on the other side is born
But Boobyclod soon drops upon the ground
A certain token that his love's unsound
While Lubberkin sticks firmly to the last
Oh were his lips to mine but joined so fast!

What you can expect:

The seed that sticks to your cheek the longest is the one you should go with. We'd advise not doing this in front of your love objects, however. (*Not only could the apple-seeds-stuck-to-the-cheeks look quench any observer's passion, but who wants to be called Boobyclod?*)

Okay, one more apple ritual, just for the heck of it.

Here's what you do:

1. Say the following words while swinging an apple paring around your head (*yeehaw!*):

I pare this pippin round and round again,
My sweetheart's name to flourish on the plain.
I fling the unbroken paring over my head,
My sweetheart's letter on the ground is read.

Again, see what shape the apple paring falls in—
it's the initial of your next sweetheart's first or last name.

Hemp Seed

SEEDS FROM THE HEMP PLANT HAVE ALWAYS HELD SPECIAL divining powers in matters of love. As Christianity spread, the pagan rituals associated with hemp didn't vanish; they merely reappeared dressed in new clothes—with their source of power attributed to various patron saints.

And let's not be coy: yes, hemp is more commonly known as cannabis, or marijuana. So immediately you can see why there is a connection between the seeds and the ability to conjure up visions.

Here is a ritual to try:

Most hemp-seed rituals are supposed to be performed on St. John's Eve, the Christian answer to Midsummer's Night Eve, also known as the summer solstice, one of the most magical and powerful nights of the pagan calendar. *(St. John's Eve is fixed on June 22 even though the exact date of the summer solstice varies slightly from year to year.)* See page 104 for more rituals associated with that day.

Hemp rituals also have traditionally worked well on other important Christian holy days such as All Saints Eve (Halloween), and Christmas Eve.

Here's what you do:

1. Get your hands on a cup or two of hemp seed. You're on your own there. But once you've scored some…

2. Go out after dark *(midnight or thereabouts is best— certainly under cover of darkness)* and sprinkle the seeds all around you and say the following three times:

Hempseed I saw
Hempseed I hoe
And he that is my true-love
Come after me and mow

What you can expect:

The idea, of course, is that you'll look behind you and see a vision of your true love, who will apparently be kneeling down and grabbing onto imaginary hemp plants, as if to harvest them. Be careful of this one! Not only should you be wary of any strangers kneeling in your yard after midnight, but apparently this ritual can present you with other, less desirable visions, such as a coffin or a black bird, which mean you will die in the coming year. Cheerful, weren't they, those medieval types?

Ashes

ON CERTAIN SAINTS' FEAST DAYS, ASHES CAN BE USED TO see visions of future romantic partners and adventures.

Here is a ritual to try: As with many of the more out-there rituals, this one seems to work best on St. John's Eve *(June 22)*. *(See page 104 for further details.)*

A fire is required for this one—there's just no way around it. If you don't have a fireplace, or you live in a neighborhood where an outdoor bonfire isn't practical, perhaps you can make do with a candle and a piece of newspaper. Don't do this around wood or other flammables or the only visions you'll be having will be through layers of white gauze.

Here's what you do:

1. Right before going to bed, smooth out the ashes of your fire *(or fire substitute)*.
2. Get up the next morning before anyone else has a chance to disturb the ashes, and look at them.

What you can expect:

Whatever appears in the ashes is what the coming year has in store for you. The outline of a wedding ring, for example, means you will get married. Or you might see something that indicates the profession of your future mate—a tooth, perhaps, if you are destined to marry a dentist *(poor you)*.

Unfortunately, you must also be prepared for the worst. Like so many divination rituals, this one may show you a coffin, or a raven, or something else that symbolized death to the medieval mind.

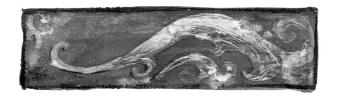

Church Accessories

Traditionally believed to drive away devils, sickness, and pain, the sound of church bells has long been used to rescue troubled romantic relationships, as has dust from Christian churches. (*Ah-choo!*)

All sorts of wonderful cures for disease and remedies for woe are attributed to church bells and other objects. Want to drive away a frightening storm? Ring the church bells. Stop the spread of a virulent flu? Ring those bells. Ensure the quick and safe delivery of your baby? Hang around a church with bells when your due date approaches. In addition, drinking water from a church bell was said to have wonderful healing properties *(just how that would work, we're not exactly sure)*. And the grease from church bells is said to prevent all sorts of disease, including shingles and heartache. Those bells run the gamut.

Most significant for our purposes, however, is the fact that church-related charms have long been used to make the course of true love run smoother.

Here are some rituals to try:

If your current relationship is floundering, and you want to try and save it, try the following bell-related ritual.

Here's what you do:

Convince your spouse or lover to take a walk on Sunday morning past a church that rings its bells at predictable hours. Contrive it so you are standing just outside the church when this happens to get the full benefit.

What you can expect:
Go get the Sunday paper and relax, already—
you've done what you can to save the relationship.

Moving on from bells, for centuries church dust was considered an essential ingredient for restoring the oomph to a love relationship. Not to mention banishing any demons that might be lurking in your household.

Here's what you do:
1. Gather a bit of dust from under the pews
   of a Catholic church, or from behind a
   statue of Mary or another saint.
   Bring a baggie or other easy-to-hide container,
   and get enough dust to fill a thimble
   (those wacky medieval measurements!).
2. Dissolve the dust in your favorite beverage. Bottoms up!

What you can expect:
More zing to your relationship
(and probably a chalky aftertaste).

Baptism Cake

CAKES MADE TO CELEBRATE INFANT BAPTISM HAVE SPECIAL divination powers in matters of the heart. In addition to taking away Original Sin, and officially welcoming the new child into the church, baptisms also have significance for would-be lovers. Most baptism love rituals are based upon the baptism cake, a baked delicacy that was eaten in celebration of the event. In the early eighteenth century a traditional baptism cake was gingerbread; another popular version was sweet currant bread.

Here's what you do:

1. Get yourself invited to a baptism, and offer to bake a cake. *(Gingerbread is tasty.)*
2. Cut the first slice of cake into small pieces and distribute to all of the single people in the room *(don't forget yourself, if appropriate).*
3. Eat the cake.

What you can expect:

That night the cake-eaters should dream of their true love.

Some versions of this ritual insist that if a boy is being baptized, the cake should be given only to the girls present; likewise, if a girl is being baptized, it should be given to just boys. Fasting is also recommended for this rite, as for so many others. Specifically, the person who wishes to induce the dream should not eat anything after the baptism "from food to food," meaning from dinner to breakfast. Hunger is a great hallucinogen.

Bible Charms

In spite of the church's staunch disapproval, people have long used the Bible to divine the future—especially in love matters. Any fan of nineteenth-century literature *(the works of Thomas Hardy or George Eliot, for example)* knows that upper-class young women of the time loved to play divination games with the household Bible. Those wacky Victorians! Although usually done in secret *(no Christian parent would approve of such activities)*, opening up a Bible at random, or dropping it on the floor, or otherwise choosing a particular passage by chance was the favorite way of discovering what the future held in terms of romance, love, and marriage.

Here are some rituals to try:

Bibles used to come with locks and keys, and the Bible key was an essential part of many of the rituals tied to romance. You should be aware that the key was used for many other rituals as well, including finding lost objects and insuring protection from illness. Since your household Bible is unlikely to have a key, we offer rituals adjusted appropriately.

Here's what you do:

1. Place the key in the Bible between the sixth and seventh verses of the last chapter of the Song of Solomon. *(This is the passage that begins "Many waters cannot quench love, neither can the floods drown it. Love is as strong as death, but jealousy is as cruel as the grave. If a man should give all the substance of his house for love, it would all be utter-*

ly consumed.") No Bible key? Use your house or car key. The bigger the key, the better *(well, easier)*, as you'll see below. You can also place your key in the Book of Ruth *(on the page that contains the famous passage beginning "Where you go I will go")*.

2. Once the key has been inserted *(as close to the gutter of the book as possible)*, close the book. Then tie it shut with a garter "taken from the right knee." Okay, so that's probably not an option, unless you've just stumbled home from the wedding reception of your best friend. We'll give you permission to use any piece of clothing that lends itself to being tied in a knot—the belt from your bathrobe, for example, or a pair of nylons. Use whatever you've found to tie the Bible closed—not too tightly, but enough to keep the key in place.

3. Here's the tricky part. Pick up the closed Bible by inserting your pinkies, one on either end of the book, into the page in the Bible that contains the key. You might need to wiggle a bit, depending on how tightly you have tied the pages together.

4. Then, hold the Bible, suspended with your pinkies, spine up, as you say the following:

If (name him or her) *be my true lover's name.*
May the Bible turn around
And the key the same

5. Try to hold the Bible in this position for 5 minutes
   (this is not easy).

What you can expect:
If it balances perfectly, you're out of luck. But if it shifts,
or even falls, you're gonna get your man or woman.

Other versions of this ritual require you to do the same thing,
only your current romantic partner lends a pinkie *(the Bible is suspended
between you)* so that both of you are told, once and for all, whether
you should get married.
  Naturally, these activities were prohibited by the church.
Still, they apparently helped while away many a long winter evening.

The Bible is also helpful when setting up a new home with
your loved one.

Here's what you do:
1. The first time you enter the house
   (or apartment, or condo), bring your Bible and
   a *new and unopened* container of salt.
2. Make sure the Bible crosses the threshold first;
   then open the package of salt and sprinkle a
   little bit in each room to ensure that you and
   your love will be happy and that your
   relationship will flourish.

(If you have time to remember in the midst of moving, you should also sprinkle some old salt in your previous dwelling once everything has been removed, and leave the old salt package there. This ensures that you are leaving any sorrow that has accumulated in the relationship behind).

What you can expect:
A fresh start.
(We really really like this one—doesn't everyone deserve the chance to try again with a clean slate?)

Saint John's Eve

MORE POPULARLY KNOWN AS MIDSUMMER'S NIGHT EVE, or the summer solstice, this was one of the most important days on the pagan calendar, and many of the rituals associated with the day address romantic love.

Falling on the summer solstice, the longest day of the year, the day's festivities were meant as thanks for summer's light and warmth, and as reminders that winter's chill and darkness were on their way. Anxious to banish pagan practices as quickly as possible, the church dubbed this day St. John's feast day, hoping that new Christians would begin thinking about spiritual matters as guided by St. John the Baptist, rather than cavorting around bonfires on forlorn hillsides. (*You've got to have a dream, after all*).

Instead, the many weird and wonderful rituals that had been in practice for centuries before Christ's birth were merely renamed in honor of the Christian saint. If some of the rituals make you uncomfortable—and they can have that effect—think of the celebration in symbolic terms: it was Saint John's mission to repel the darkness of spiritual ignorance, and you can take this "white magic" associated with him in the same spirit.

Here are some rituals to try:

There are too many love-related folk rituals associated with St. John to list them all here, but we've provided a few of our favorites.

Want to get hitched? One honored St. John's Eve tradition follows. It was originally intended for girls, but we say: boys, too.

Here's what you do:
Dance around a St. John's bonfire before midnight *(perhaps an outdoor barbeque will suffice)*.

What you can expect:
To get married within a year.

In sixteenth century rural England, there was apparently a brief time when the church acquiesced to this folk tradition: the local priest led a formal procession from the church up to the site of the bonfire *(usually on the highest hill in the region)* and lit the sacred fire while blessing it. *(Hey, if you can't beat 'em, join 'em.)*

Another fire-related ritual
(and most of the St. John's Eve rituals do involve fire, which in pagan times was in honor of the god Baal) is as follows:

Here's what you do:
Dance around the bonfire, then leap over the flames. Careful!

What you can expect:
Protection from heartbreak for an entire year. And if you do this with a romantic partner, your relationship will flourish during the following twelve months. *(There are also a lot of bonuses for doing this fire dancing and leaping that have nothing to do with love. The pagan version of snake oil, it's good for everything you can think of—warding off*

devils, exorcising evil spirits, protecting the health of your livestock, etc. It seems it was the best general pick-me-up those medieval types had to offer.)

Here's a non-fire-related ritual.

Here's what you do:

Dig a little hole in the ground, preferably at the intersection of two or three roads, in darkness and after midnight. The next day, in broad daylight, put your ear to the hole and listen.

What you can expect:

You will hear a whisper that tells you your future spouse's profession. *(Perhaps you should have an excuse handy, should anyone be curious as to what you are doing: "I lost a contact!" or "Just watching this interesting bug").*

Easter

The day on which Christians the world-over celebrate the resurrection of Jesus is also rife with a host of love traditions—many of dubious origin.

Although ostensibly linked to the high spiritual significance of the day, a number of love rituals from pagan times are now celebrated at Easter. One of the stranger rituals originated in thirteenth century England. It should be performed on the two days following Easter—Easter Monday and Easter Tuesday—and involves the ritual beating of men by women, and women by men. On Monday, men get to hit their spouse or sweetheart with a whip made of hay or straw; on Tuesday, women get to return the favor. What does this signify? Beats us. Other versions of this ritual instruct the men to steal a particular object from the object of their affection—a handkerchief, for example—on Monday. Then the women contrive to steal their property back on Tuesday. Ah, young love.

FYI, if you were one of those who always got a new outfit for Easter Sunday, that practice likely started with Roman emperor Constantine (A.D. 325), who ordered everyone in his domain to wear their best clothes on this holiest of holy days. Ever since then, it has been considered good luck to wear at least one new item of clothing on Easter. *(We also think this dolling up bit probably had something to do with pheromones; after all, Easter usually falls at the beginning of spring, when a young man's—or woman's—fancy turns toward love.)*

A Medieval English rhyme sums it up:

*On Easter let your clothes be new
Or else be sure you will it rue*

Here's what you do:
Buy that new bonnet.

What you can expect:
Good luck.

May

The month of May traditionally has been devoted to venerating the Virgin Mary, but a number of pagan beliefs cling to it as well.

Going a'maying used to be synonymous with joyful frolicking in meadows, picking flowers for May baskets, and in general dancing and singing as an homage to the Roman goddess Maia, mother of Mercury. It was also for centuries an excuse for indulging in all sorts of clandestine excess: trysts in the woods, cross-dressing, drunkenness…you get the idea. The church tried to channel as much of this frivolity as it could into more legitimate channels, specifically honoring Mary, Jesus's mother, but nothing could squelch the high spirits that emerged around this time of year. Spring fever, anyone?

Here are some rituals to try:
It is considered unlucky to get married in May, *("Marry in May, rue for aye," goes one ancient warning.)* We cannot tell you why— the reason has been lost over the centuries. Perhaps this is why we consider it good luck today to be a "June bride."

Here's a charming English rhyme that sets out the rules for when to marry. Most of the special days and festivals referred to are no longer observed, but it will help you get the gist:

Advent marriage doth deny
But Hilary gives thee liberty.
Septuagesima says thee nay,
Eight days from Easter says you may
Rogation bids thee to contain
But Trinity sets thee free again.

Here's what you do:

1. Well, actually, what you *don't* do is get married in May. What you *can* do is get up early and gather dew on the first day of the month. How do you "gather" dew? Excellent question! We're going on the assumption that you collect blades of grass and leaves and flowers on which dew has accumulated. If you find a better way, please let us know.

2. Then, throw the dew over your shoulder. *(Yes, throw it—that's what the experts say. But it is probably more like sprinkling than throwing.)*

What you can expect:

A happy marriage.

In some parts of eastern Europe, unmarried girls used to wash their faces in dew before sunrise on May 1, then name the man they wished to marry. A vision shortly followed this refreshing activity. If you guys can drag yourself out of bed, you might be given a vision, too.

BUT HERE'S A STERN WARNING: other versions of the May dew ritual thing say that anyone who washes their face in dew on a May morning will marry the first person she meets. So be careful of your creepy neighbor who gets up early to walk his dog.

For those of you who need a little restorative, May dew is also very good for the complexion, as this old English rhyme reminds us:

The fair maid who the first of May
Goes to the fields at break of day
And washes in dew from the hawthorne tree,
Will ever after handsome be.

Shrove Tuesday

The week before Lent begins has long been a time to cut loose. The festivities peak on Shrove Tuesday, the day before Ash Wednesday, after which all good Christians must renounce pleasure for fasting and prayer in preparation for the Resurrection of Christ on Easter Sunday.

Shrove Tuesday is more commonly known as Fat Tuesday in New Orleans, Carnival in Rio, and myriad other names around the world. But whatever you call it, it has long been one of those rare get-out-of-jail-free cards dealt to normally temperate Christians. Today, the most solidly Catholic regions of the world tend to be the ones most famous for excessive Shrove Tuesday revelries.

During Carnival, anything goes, and it usually does. First observed in Roman times, the wild carryings-on involved everything from excessive eating and drinking, to the wearing of frightening or grotesque costumes, to sexual promiscuity and thievery.

Interestingly enough, to shrive means, according to the *American Heritage Dictionary*, "to hear the confession of and give absolution to a penitent." Historically the fun didn't begin on Shrove Tuesday until after an early-morning confession. The idea was that your soul would then be clean in preparation for Lent. Fat chance. The idea that deprivation is just around the corner seems instead to spur most people in the opposite direction. Party on!

Many Shrove Tuesday rituals involve pancakes. This goes back so far that no one is quite sure how it began. It has been suggested, however, that medieval kitchens needed to get rid of the lard and by-products derived from cooking meat since meat was forbidden during Lent *(today Catholics are supposed to refrain from eating meat on Fridays only)*. Shrove Tuesday was the last day to cleanse the kitchen of any meat-related food. Although today that wouldn't immediately make us think "pancakes!", traditionally they were made and fried in lard, so it must have been a tasty way to rid yourself of any such excess. Pancake-throwing was also apparently one of the highlights of Shrove Tuesday, as was cockfighting and other somewhat violent sports.

So what does all this have to do with love? Not much, if you're mostly concerned with commitment and long-term relationships. But if you're not quite ready to settle down, Shrove Tuesday is your day to party.

Here's what you do:

1. Invite your friends over—as early as you can manage.
2. Make a huge stack of pancakes. But here's the important part: the first pancake you make must be shared by everyone. So make it a big one—fill the whole pan with batter. Give everyone at least a bite.

What you can expect:

When you and your friends go out to play later that day everyone who had a bit of pancake will have extraordinary luck flirting and otherwise having great lascivious romantic adventures.

Here's a related couplet from Merry Olde England, circa 1600. Try not to be offended by the judgmental language.

> Maids, fritters and pancakes enough
>   see you make;
> Let the sluts have one pancake,
>   for company's sake.

Valentine's Day

Everyone knows that Valentine's Day is for lovers. It is also the only saint's feast day still appearing on secular calendars around the world. But few people know the whole Valentine story or have heard about the more obscure love rituals traditionally performed on this day.

The association of Valentine with rites related to romance is due to the largely futile efforts of early religious Christian leaders to do away with pagan festivals by substituting Christian observances and hoping for the best. Originally February 14 was the Roman festival of youth, Lupercalia, sacred to Juno, the Queen of Heaven and protector of women. Juno, wife of Jupiter, was said to bestow her blessing on courtship rituals or marriages celebrated that day, and to give girls good luck when playing romantic games of chance *(sweethearts were often drawn by lottery)*. Another pagan connection between Valentine and romance is that birds were believed to choose their mates for the season in mid-February, close to the feast of St. Valentine.

Rather than banishing these pagan practices in favor of more spiritual pursuits, early Christians merely moved all their existing matchmaking activities, lock, stock, and barrel, to fall under St. Valentine's patronage. *(There is little evidence that any real St. Valentine existed, although three different early saints are contenders for that honor. See page 22.)* The church tried numerous times to quash the romantic games in the seventeenth century; even St. Francis de Sales put his influence into the effort—but to no avail. Hallmark cheered.

Here are some rituals to try:

In Shakespeare's time, women would "challenge" men on St. Valentine's by trying to be the first to say "Good morning, it's Valentine's Day" to the man of their choice. Any unmarried man challenged like this would have to comply. We're not sure what happened if the man was unwilling, but much of the old literature on St. Valentine's Day included admonitions to stay inside if you didn't want to get ensnared by a member of the opposite sex. The only thing we know for sure is that the man was required to give the woman a present as a result of her challenge.

Here's what you do:

Pin five bay leaves to your pillow:
one in each corner and one in the middle,
on the night before Valentine's Day.

What you can expect:

That night you will dream of your true love.

Childermass

HOLY INNOCENTS' DAY (DECEMBER 28), OR CHILDERMASS as it is called in England, commemorates the young boys in Bethlehem who, according to the Gospel of Matthew, died under King Herod's edict that all boys under two years old be killed, in his attempt to destroy the Christ child.

Yes, it's always been a fun day. In medieval England, young boys were reminded of the Herod story by being beaten. Lovely! In addition, it has long been considered a day on which you will have particularly horrid luck if you try to accomplish anything important. This belief was taken so seriously that the coronation of Edward IV of England was delayed because it would have fallen on Childermass. It is considered *especially* bad luck to begin any task, project, or endeavor on this day.

Including getting married. Indeed, in England, marriages were traditionally banned on Childermass lest they end in misery or disaster.

Here's what you do (or not do, as the case may be).
Even if you've been hit by the post-Christmas blues, are desperate to score a date for New Year's Eve, or otherwise are feeling vulnerable in the romance department, we recommend being safe rather than sorry. So on December 28, don't go on any first dates, don't approach that guy you met at your sister-in-law's, and don't call up that woman from Accounting, even though sparks were flying at the company holiday party. Just take a cold shower, and put everything on hold until December 29. *(This is an* excellent *time to hole up in your bed under a down comforter with the latest supermarket thriller, eating Fritos.)*
Tomorrow will be another, better day. There. Was that so hard?

Advent

IN THE SAME WAY THAT LENT IS THE
preparation for Easter, Advent is the preparation
for Christmas. It begins on the fourth Sunday
before Christmas.

Here are some rituals to try:

There are numerous love rituals specifically meant
to be performed during the Advent season, including
some that reveal not only the name of your future
spouse *(like so many other rituals)*, but his or her *character*.
(Intriguing, no?) We have yet to find any rational
explanation for this, but William Walsh in his book
Curiosities of Popular Customs confirms the fact that "many
quaint and peculiar observances" have long been
performed during this time. *(One favorite of ours has nothing
to do with love, being a ritual "exorcism" of mice, moles, and caterpillars
from gardens that have been harvested recently, and will be replanted after
the new year.)*

Here's what you can do:

Go to a woodpile. *(If you don't have one, try going to a wooded area that
has leaves and twigs scattered on the ground.)* Close your eyes, and draw
out *(or pick up)* the first stick that your hand touches.

What you can expect:
If the stick is straight, your spouse will be kind, gentle, and honest. If crooked, you may want to rethink your plans.

An old English rhyme summarizes it as follows:

If it straight and even be, and
have no knots at all
A gentle husband then will surely to them fall
But if it crooked be, and knotted
here and there
A crabbed, churlish husband then they
earnestly do fear

Can't decide between admirers? Try this. It takes time, but if your suitors aren't pushing you for an immediate answer, go for it.

Here's what you can do:
1. Take an onion and scratch the names of your current *(or potential)* lovers in it.
2. Put it near a fire. *(Again, be creative if you have no fireplace. A heating vent or radiator should work.)*
3. Keep an eye on the onion over the next week or two.

What you can expect:

Eventually, the onion will sprout roots in the scratched out areas—watch closely to see which name sprouts first. You might also invest in a case of Glade, or perform this ritual in a room that isn't used very often, as the smell will get pungent.

An old British rhyme explains how it works:

Four onions, five, or eight, they take,
    and make in every one
Such names as they do fancy most and
    best do think upon
Thus near the chimney them they set,
    and that same onion than
That first doth sprout, doth surely bear
    the name of their good man/woman.

All Saints Day

ON ALL SAINTS DAY EVE—more commonly referred to as Halloween—there are a number of things you can do other than ring doorbells and beg for candy *(or, for those of you past the costume stage, steal from the bags of younger or more naïve household members)*. You'll be surprised by how many rituals for curing love's ills are associated with this day.

Here are some rituals to try:

According to many world religions, this is the one night of the year in which the spirit—Christians would say "spiritual"—world is closest to the world of the living. There are more myths, legends, and superstitions connected with this night than can be related here, but it is worth mentioning that of all the ancient festivals still in practice, Halloween brings together the oddest and most peculiar bedfellows imaginable. Pagan, druidic, and Christian beliefs don't collide as much as melt together. And along with all the other supernatural manifestations that can happen, this is one of the most powerful nights in the year for divination. Naturally, many people have taken advantage of this in order to foretell their future love *(or lack thereof)*.

Here's what you do:

1. To check on the faithfulness of an existing romantic partner, take two nuts and place them side by side by the fire.
   (Gas burner? Outdoor barbeque? You might need to be creative here.)
   The important thing is that the heat source be hot enough to roast the nuts.

2. Name the nuts, one for each partner.
   Then sit back and relax.

What you can expect:
If a nut roasts quietly and predictably,
then that nut *(person)* will be faithful and true.
If it cracks or jumps, that person will be unfaithful.

You can do a variation of this ritual in which you gather up
a bunch of nuts, and name each one for potential romantic
partners. Throw them into the fire one by one. Which one
burns the most spectacularly? That's the person with whom
you will have the most passionate relationship.

Here's an old Irish tradition:

Here's what you do:
Throw a ball of yarn out of the window
(holding on to the end of it, of course).
Then rewind it slowly,
while saying a Paternoster *(Our Father).*

What you can expect:
Sometime during this process you will have
a vision of your future mate.

And yet another ritual.

Here's what you do.

1. Buy or gather from your garden two long-stemmed red roses. A big caveat here: you cannot speak from the time you acquire the roses until you get home and into the privacy of your bedroom.

2. After getting home with the roses, go to your bedroom *(remember: don't speak to anyone)*. Kneel beside your bed. Name one rose for yourself, and the other for your desired romantic partner. Twine together the stems of the roses *(this is why they have to be long-stemmed)* while saying the following:

> *Twine, twine, and intertwine*
> *Let my love be wholly mine.*
> *If his heart be kind and true,*
> *Deeper grow his rose's hue.*

What you can expect:

As you can probably guess from the rhyme, if your love is true, the rose named after your partner will turn a deeper shade of red.

Here's one last ritual that frankly seems quite weird.

Here's what you do:

1. Put a glass of water by your bedside.
2. Then, put a sliver of wood into the glass of water.

What you can expect:

During the night, you will have a dream that you are falling off a bridge (!). If your lover is true, he will magically appear and save you just before you hit the water. We couldn't find any information about what happens if your lover is not true. But if it's what we suspect, just repeat to yourself, "This is only a dream."